James Gillespie Birney

The American Churches the Bulwarks of American Slavery

Third American Edition

James Gillespie Birney

The American Churches the Bulwarks of American Slavery
Third American Edition

ISBN/EAN: 9783744732871

Printed in Europe, USA, Canada, Australia, Japan

Cover: Foto ©Lupo / pixelio.de

More available books at **www.hansebooks.com**

THE

AMERICAN CHURCHES

THE BULWARKS

OF

AMERICAN SLAVERY.

BY JAMES G. BIRNEY.

THIRD AMERICAN EDITION.

REVISED BY THE AUTHOR.

Concord, N. H.
PUBLISHED BY PARKER PILLSBURY.
1885.

INTRODUCTION.

BY PARKER PILLSBURY.

The following work is reproduced without apology. It is needed as authentic anti-slavery history, and as showing beyond all dispute who were most zealous defenders of American slavery, and the most virulent opponents of the active abolitionists.

The author, Hon. James G. Birney, the only truly anti-slavery man ever nominated for the presidency while slavery lasted, was a native of Kentucky, and connected both by birth and marriage with many of its first families. His education completed, he spent fifteen years in Huntsville, Alabama, a successful lawyer, and for a time solicitor-general, besides being tendered a seat on the bench of the supreme court.

He was appointed by the legislature to nominate, at his sole discretion, the faculty of the State University. Returning to Kentucky, he was called to the Professorship of Political Economy, Rhetoric, and Belles-Lettres in Centre College at Danville in that state. And those who knew him testified that "his character and Christian influence were quite equal to his public standing." But public and private virtues, intellectual eminence, and the highest lay official positions in the Presbyterian church, were all lost in becoming a repentant slaveholder and an active, earnest abolitionist.

About the commencement of the wondrous career of William Lloyd Garrison and the establishment by him of *The Liberator* in Boston, Mr. Theodore D. Weld, one of our most eloquent and powerful anti-slavery lecturers and writers, encountered Mr. Birney while yet a slaveholder, and held some searching discussions with him and his minister, also a slaveholder, on the right of one man to hold absolute property in his fellow-man. The argument began with the minister in the absence of Birney, who welcomed Weld to the parsonage till he should return. He came in a few days, and then the minister invited him and another lawyer to meet Weld at dinner at his house.

Here, also, the right of property in man problem was in order. But to the stunning surprise of the minister, he learned that Birney was already fully convinced, intellectually, that only the right of the kidnapper could be urged for holding such property ; and that kidnapped human chattels could never be owned, or held as lawful possessions, though sanctified by transfer and conveyance through a thousand generations !

The discussion continued, earnest and more earnest, all day and evening, even the minister's wife leaning to the Birney side; tea was had and drank; and at a late hour Mr. Birney invited Weld to dinner next day with him, and to come to his office in the morning. And he went in the morning and found his host in profound meditation, sitting alone in the inner office, and ready to confess that he had slept only little the past night, but that he was fully assured of his duty, and that his slaves must have their freedom, then numbering, as Mr. Weld now thinks, forty-two.

Mr. Birney had for some years been giving much thought to the African colonization system. He had even accepted an agency in that iniquitous and slavery devised and slavery cherished enterprise, his field of operations including five of the large slaveholding states. But he soon found himself laboring in the interest of a movement adapted and intended to perpetuate the very curse he himself deplored, and was working, as he supposed, to destroy.

So, having already liberated his slaves, and generously provided for their well-being and well-doing so far as he was able, he espoused the cause of "immediate and unconditional emancipation," and by purse, pen, and voice commenced its proclamation. Driven from his native state for his anti-slavery fidelity, he crossed over into Ohio and established an anti-slavery newspaper. But he was repeatedly mobbed, his press, types, paper, and other office property being taken out and sunk in the Ohio river, the city authorities in large numbers evidently sanctioning, as did many of the church officials actually sanctify by their presence and approval, the shameful outrages. A well filled pamphlet now before me, printed at the time and on the spot, fully warrants all these statements.

The following is a specimen of the handbills that placarded the bulletin boards and walls:

"*A Fugitive from Justice.*" *100 Dollars Reward!*

The above sum will be paid for the delivery of one James G. Birney, a fugitive from justice, now abiding in the city of Cincinnati. Said Birney, in all his associations and feelings, is *black*, although his external appearance is white. The above reward will be paid, and no questions asked, by

Old Kentucky.

This was posted on a Sunday morning. The next day the Cincinnati *Whig* said, editorially,—

"*Public Sentiment.* We are informed on indisputable authority that a large number of boarders have left the Franklin House in this city; have left it on account of the reception of Mr. Birney, Editor of the Philanthropist as a boarder. There is no doubt an overwhelming majority in the city are opposed to the wild schemes of the abolitionists."

The proceedings of some of the "anti-abolition meetings," as they were named, showed that they were disgraceful as well as unlawful assemblies, though called and conducted by the authorities and best citizens. One committee, appointed to draft resolutions, contained thirteen men who were members of Episcopal, Methodist Episcopal, Wesleyan Methodist, Swedenborgian, and Unitarian churches. So was Mr. Birney regarded and rewarded by his fellow-citizens and fellow-*Christians*, only for liberating and providing for his slaves, and then becoming a faithful abolitionist! Only that and nothing more! He had experience enough with the churches and clergy to fully warrant the title of his little book, as all who read it will believe without more argument.

Whoever would see more on the subject, on the whole matter of Slavery and Anti-Slavery as existing in the country forty years ago, are respectfully referred to *Acts of the Anti-Slavery Apostles,* by Parker Pillsbury, to be had of him at Concord, N. H., price one dollar and fifty cents.

Publisher's Notice.

This work is reproduced by Parker Pillsbury, Concord, N. H.: price, single copy, 15 cents; 2 copies, 25 cents; 10 copies, 1 dollar.

Also, for sale, "Acts of the Anti-Slavery Apostles," by Parker Pillsbury: price, postage paid, one dollar and fifty cents.

AMERICAN SLAVERY.

THE extent to which most of the churches in America
are involved in the guilt of supporting the slave system
is known to but few in this country.* So far from being
even suspected by the great mass of the religious community here, it would not be believed but on the most indisputable evidence. Evidence of this character it is proposed
now to present—applying to the Methodist Episcopal, the
Baptist, the Presbyterian, and the Protestant Episcopal
churches. It is done with a single view to make the
British Christian public acquainted with the real state of
the case—in order that it may in the most intelligent and
effective manner exert the influence it possesses with the
American churches to persuade them to purify themselves
from a sin that has greatly debased them, and that threat-
ens in the end wholly to destroy them.

The following *memoranda* will assist English readers
in more readily apprehending the force and scope of the
evidence.

I. Of the twenty-six American states, thirteen are
slave states. Of the latter, Maryland, Virginia, Kentucky,
Missouri, and Tennessee (in part), are slave-*selling* states;
the states south of them are slave-*buying* and slave-*con-
suming* states.

II. Between the slave-selling and slave-buying states
the slave-trade is carried on extensively and systemati-
cally. The slave-trader, on completing his purchases for
a single adventure, brings the gang together at a conven-
ient point; confines the men in double rows to a large
chain running between the rows, by means of smaller lat-
eral chains tightly riveted around the wrists of the slaves,

---

* England—where this pamphlet was first published.

and connected with the principal chain. They are in this way driven along the highways (the small boys, the women, and girls following), without any release from their chains till they arrive at the ultimate place of sale. Here they occupy barracoons, till they are disposed of, one by one, or in lots, to those who will give most for them.

III. Ministers and office-bearers, and members of churches are slaveholders—buying and selling slaves (not as the regular slave-trader), but as their convenience or interest may from time to time require. As a general rule, the itinerant preachers in the Methodist church are not permitted to hold slaves—but there are frequent exceptions to the rule, especially of late.

IV. There are in the United States, about 2,487,113 slaves, and 386,069 *free people of color*. Of the slaves, 80,000 are members of the Methodist church; 80,000 of the Baptist; and about 40,000 of the other churches. These church members have no exemption from being sold by their owners as other slaves are. Instances are not rare of slaveholding members of churches selling slaves who are members of the same church with themselves. And members of churches have followed the business of slave-auctioneers.

V. In most of the slave states the master is not permitted formally to emancipate, unless the emancipated person be removed from the state (which makes the formal act unnecessary), or, unless by a special act of the legislature. If, however, he disregard the law, and permit the slave to go at liberty and "do" for himself, the law—on the theory that every slave ought to have a master to *see to him*—directs him to be sold for the benefit of the state. Instances of this, however, must be very rare. The people are better than their laws—for the writer, during a residence of more than thirty years in the slave states, never knew an instance of such a sale, nor has he ever heard of one that was fully proved to have taken place.

VI. There is no law in any of the slave states forbidding the slaveholder to remove his slaves to a free state ; nor against his giving the slaves themselves a "pass" for that purpose. The laws of some of the *free* states present obstructions to the settlement of colored persons within their limits—but these obstructions are not insurmountable, and if the validity of the laws should be tried in the tribunals, it would be found they are unconstitutional.

VII. In the slave states a slave cannot be a witness in any case, civil or criminal, in which a white is a party. Neither can a free colored person, except in Louisiana. Ohio, Indiana, and Illinois (free states), make colored persons incompetent as witnesses in any case in which a white is a party. In Ohio, a white person can prove his own ("book") account, not exceeding a certain sum, by his own oath or affirmation. A colored person cannot, as against a white. In Ohio the laws regard all who are mulattoes, or above the grade of mulattoes, as *white*.

VIII. There is no law in the slave states forbidding the several church authorities making slaveholding an offence, for which those guilty of it might be excluded from membership.

The Society of Friends exists in the slave states—it excludes slaveholders.

The United Brethren exist as a church in Maryland and Virginia, slave states. Their Annual Conference for these two states (in which are thirty preachers) met in February [1840]. The following is an extract from its minutes :—

"No charge is preferred against any (preachers) except Franklin Echard and Moses Michael.

"It appeared in evidence that Moses Michael was the owner of a female slave, which is contrary to the discipline of our church. Conference therefore resolved, that unless brother Michael manumit or set free such slave in six months, he no longer be considered a member of our church."

IX. When ecclesiastical councils excuse themselves from acting for the removal of slavery from their respective communions by saying, they cannot *legislate* for the abolition of slavery ; that slavery is a *civil* or *political* institution ; that it " belongs to Cæsar," and not to the church to put an end to it,—they shun the point at issue. To the church member who is a debauchee, a drunkard, a seducer. a murderer, they find no difficulty in saying,— "We cannot indeed proceed against your person. or your property—*this* belongs to Cæsar, to the *tribunals* of the country, to the *legislature;* but we can suspend or wholly cut you off from the communion of the church, with a view to your repentance and its purification." If a white member should by force or intimidation, day after day, deprive another white member of his property, the authorities of the churches would expel him from their body, should he refuse to make restitution or reparation, although it could not be *enforced* except through the tribunals, over which they have no control. There is, then, nothing to prevent these authorities from saying to the slave-holder, "Cease being a slaveholder and remain in the church, or continue a slaveholder and go out of it. You have your choice."

X. The slave states make it penal to teach the slaves to read. So also some of them to teach the *free colored people* to read. Thus a free colored parent may suffer the penalty for teaching his own children to read even the Scriptures. None of the slave-holding churches, or religious bodies, so far as is known, have, at any time, remonstrated with the legislatures against this iniquitous legislation, or petitioned for its repeal or modification. Nor have they reproved or questioned such of their members, as, being also members of the legislatures, sanctioned such legislation by their votes.

XI. There is no systematic instruction of the slave-members of churches, either orally or in any other way.

XII. Uniting with a church makes no change in the condition of slaves *at home.* They are thrown back just as before, among their old associates, and subjected to their corrupting influences.

XIII. But little pains are taken to secure their attendance at public worship on Sundays.

XIV. The "house-servants" are rarely present at family worship; the "field-hands," never.

XV. It is only here and there who seems to have any intelligent views of the nature of Christianity, or of a future life.

XVI. In the Methodist, Baptist, Presbyterian, and Episcopal churches, the colored people, during service, sit in a particular part of the house, now generally known as the *negro pew.* They are not permitted to sit in any other, nor to hire or purchase pews as other people, nor would they be permitted to sit, even if invited, in the pews of white persons. This applies to all colored persons, whether *members* or not, and even to *licensed ministers* of their respective connections. The "negro pew" is almost as rigidly kept up in the free states as in the slave.

XVII. In some of the older slave states, as Virginia and South Carolina, churches, in their *corporate* character, hold slaves, who are generally hired out for the support of the minister. The following is taken from the Charleston Courier of February 12th, 1835.

FIELD NEGROES, *by Thomas Gadsden.*

On Tuesday, the 17th instant, will be sold, at the north of the Exchange, at ten o'clock, a prime gang of ten NEGROES, accustomed to the culture of cotton and provisions, belonging to the INDEPENDENT CHURCH, in *Christ's Church Parish.* . . *Feb.* 6.

XVIII. Nor are instances wanting in which negroes are *bequeathed* for the benefit of the Indians, as the following Chancery notice, taken from a Savannah (Geo.) paper will show.

" *Bryan Superior Court.*

Between John J. Maxwell and others, Executors of
   Ann Pray, complainants, and   IN
Mary Sleigh and others, Devisees and Legatees, under   EQUITY.
   the will of Ann Pray, defendants.

"A Bill having been filed for the distribution of the estate of the Testatrix, Ann Pray, and it appearing that among other legacies in her will, is the following, viz., a legacy of one fourth of certain negro slaves to the American Board of Commissioners for Domestic [Foreign it probably should have been] Missions, for the purpose of sending the gospel to the heathen, and particularly to the Indians of this continent. It is on motion of the solicitors of the complainants ordered, that all persons claiming the said legacy, do appear and answer the bill of the complainants, within four months from this day. And it is ordered that this order be published in a public Gazette of the city of Savannah, and in one of the Gazettes of Philadelphia, once a month for four months.

" Extract from the minutes, Dec. 2nd, 1832.

"JOHN SMITH, C. S. C. B. C."—(The bequest was not accepted.)

INFLUENCES UNDER WHICH THE AMERICAN CHURCHES HAVE BEEN BROUGHT.

Charleston (City) Gazette.—" We protest againt the assumption —the unwarrantable assumption—that slavery is ultimately to be extirpated from the Southern states. Ultimate abolitionists are enemies of the South, the same in kind, and only less in degree, than immediate abolitionists."

Washington (City) Telegraph.—"As a man, a Christian, and a citizen, we believe that slavery is right; that the condition of the slaveholding states is the best existing organization of civil society."

Chancellor Harper, of South Carolina.—"It is the order of nature, and of GOD, that the being of superior faculties and knowledge, and therefore of superior power, should control and dispose of those who are inferior. It is as much in the order of nature that men should enslave each other, as that *other* animals should prey upon each other."

Columbia (S. C.) Telescope.—"Let us declare, through the public journals of our country, that the question of slavery is not, and shall not be open to discussion; that the system is deep-rooted among us, and must remain forever; that the very moment any private individual attempts to lecture upon its evils and immorality, and the necessity of putting means in operation to secure us from them, in the same moment his tongue shall be cut out and cast upon a dunghill."

Augusta (Geo.) Chronicle.—"He [Amos Dresser] should have been hung up as high as Haman, to rot upon the gibbet, until the wind whistled through his bones. The cry of the whole South should be death, INSTANT DEATH, to the abolitionist, wherever he is caught."

[Amos Dresser, now a missionary in Jamaica, was a theological student at Lane Seminary, near Cincinnati. In the vacation (August, 1835) he undertook to sell Bibles in the state of Tennessee, with a view to raise means further to continue his studies. Whilst there, he fell under suspicion of being an abolitionist, was arrested by the Vigilance Committee, whilst attending a religious meeting in the neighborhood of Nashville, the capital of the state, and after an afternoon and evening's inquisition condemned to receive twenty lashes on his naked body. The sentence was executed on him, between eleven and twelve o'clock on Saturday night, in the presence of most of the committee, and of an infuriated and blaspheming mob. The Vigilance Committee (an unlawful association) consisted of sixty persons. Of these, twenty-seven were members of churches; one, a religious teacher, another, the elder, who but a few days before, in the Presbyterian church, handed Mr. Dresser the bread and wine at the communion of the Lord's Supper.]

In the latter part of the summer of 1835, the slaveholders generally became alarmed at the progress of the abolitionists. Meetings were held throughout the South to excite all classes of people to the requisite degree of exasperation against them. At one of these meetings, held at Clinton, Mississippi, it was

Resolved,—

"That slavery through the South and West is not felt as an evil, moral or political, but it is recognized in reference to the *actual*, and not to any Utopian condition of our slaves, as a blessing, both to master and slave."

Resolved,—

"That it is our decided opinion, that any individual who dares to circulate, with a view to effectuate the designs of the abolitionists, any of the incendiary tracts or newspapers now in a course of transmission to this country, is justly worthy, in the sight of God and man, of immediate death ; and we doubt not that such would be the punishment of any such offender in any part of the state of Mississippi where he may be found."

Resolved,—

"That we recommend to the citizens of Mississippi, to encourage the cause of the American Colonization Society, so long as in good faith it concentrates its energies alone on the removal of the free people of color out of the United States."

Resolved,—

"That the clergy of the state of Mississippi be hereby recommended at once to take a stand upon this subject, and that their further silence in relation thereto, at this crisis, will, in our opinion, be subject to serious censure."

At Charleston, South Carolina, the post-office was forced, the Anti-Slavery publications, which were there for distribution or further transmission to *masters*, taken out and made a bonfire of in the street, by a mob of several thousand people.

A public meeting was appointed to be held a few days afterward to complete, in the same spirit in which they were commenced, preparations for excluding Anti-Slavery publications from circulation, and for ferreting out persons suspected of favoring the doctrines of the abolitionists, that they might be subjected to lynch law. At this assembly the *Charleston Courier* informs us,—

"The Clergy of all denominations attended in a body, lending their sanction to the proceedings, and adding by their presence to the impressive character of the scene."

It was there resolved,—

"That the thanks of this meeting are due to the Reverend gentlemen of the clergy in this city, who have so promptly and so effectually responded to public sentiment, by suspending their schools in which the *free colored population* were taught; and that this meeting deem it a patriotic action, worthy of all praise, and proper to be imitated by other teachers of similar schools throughout the state."

The alarm of the Virginia slaveholders was not less— nor were the clergy in the city of Richmond, the capital, less prompt than the clergy in Charleston to respond to "public sentiment." Accordingly, on the 29th of July, they assembled together, and

Resolved, *unanimously*,—

"That we earnestly deprecate the unwarrantable and highly improper interference of the people of any other state with the domestic relations of master and slave.

"That the example of our Lord Jesus Christ and his apostles, in not interfering with the question of slavery, but uniformly recognizing the relations of master and servant, and giving full and affectionate instruction to both, is worthy of the imitation of all ministers of the gospel.

"That we will not patronize nor receive any pamphlet or newspaper of the Anti-Slavery Societies, and that we will discountenance the circulation of all such papers in the community.

"That the suspicions which have prevailed to a considerable extent against ministers of the gospel and professors of religion in the state of Virginia, as identified with abolitionists, are *wholly unmerited*—believing as we do, from extensive acquaintance with our churches and brethren, that they are unanimous in opposing the pernicious schemes of abolitionists."

THE METHODIST EPISCOPAL CHURCH.
700,000 Members.

In 1780, four years before the Episcopal Methodist Church was regularly organized in the United States, the conference bore the following testimony against slavery:

"The conference acknowledges that slavery is contrary to the laws of God, man, and nature, and hurtful to society; contrary to the dictates of conscience and true religion, and doing what we would not others should do unto us."

In 1784, when the church was fully organized, rules were adopted, prescribing the times at which members, who were already slaveholders, should emancipate their slaves. These rules were succeeded by the following:

"Every person concerned, who will not comply with these rules, shall have liberty quietly to withdraw from our society within the twelve months following the notice being given us aforesaid; otherwise the assistants shall exclude him the society.

"No person holding slaves shall in future be admitted into society, or to the Lord's Supper, till he previously comply with these rules concerning slavery.

"Those who buy, sell, or give [slaves] away, unless on purpose to free them, shall be expelled immediately."

In 1785 the following language was held :—

" We do hold in the deepest abhorrence the practice of slavery, and shall not cease to seek its destruction by all wise and prudent means."

In 1801 :—

" We declare that we are more than ever convinced of the great evil of African slavery. which still exists in these United States."

" Every member of the society who sells a slave shall, immediately after full proof. be excluded from the society, &c."

" The Annual Conferences are directed to draw up addresses for the gradual emancipation of the slaves to the legislature." " Proper committees shall be appointed by the Annual Conferences, out of the most respectable of our friends, for the conducting of the business ; and the presiding elders, deacons, and travelling preachers, shall procure as many proper signatures as possible to the addresses, and give all the assistance in their power, in every respect to aid the committees, and to further the blessed undertaking. Let this be continued from year to year until the desired end be accomplished."

In 1836 the General Conference met in May, in Cincinnati, a town of 46,000 inhabitants, and the metropolis of the free state of Ohio. An anti-slavery society had been formed there a year or two before. A meeting of the society was appointed for the evening of the 10th of May, to which the abolitionists attending the Conference as delegates were invited.* Of those who attended, two of them made remarks suitable to the occasion. On the 12th of May, Rev. S. G. Roszell presented in the conference the following preamble and resolutions :—

" Whereas great excitement has pervaded this country on the subject of modern abolitionism, which is reported to have been increased in this city recently by the unjustifiable conduct of two members of the General Conference in lecturing upon, and in favor of that agitating topic ;—and whereas, such a course on the part of any of its members is calculated to bring upon this body the suspicion and distrust of the community. and misrepresent its sentiments in regard to the point at issue ;—and whereas, in this aspect of the case, a due regard for its own character, as well as a just concern for the interests of the church confided to its care, demand a full, decided, and unequivocal expression of the views of the General Conference in the premises." Therefore,

---

* The Rev. Mr. Lovejoy, who was afterwards slain by the mob in defending his press at Alton, Illinois, was present at the meeting. He was on his way from St. Louis, where he then resided, to Pittsburg, to attend the General Assembly of the Presbyterian Church.

1. Resolved,—

" By the delegates of the Annual Conference in General Conference assembled, that they disapprove in the most unqualified sense, the conduct of the two members of the General Conference who are reported to have lectured in this city recently, upon, and in favor of, modern abolitionism."

2. Resolved,—

" By the delegates of the Annual Conferences in General Conference assembled,—that they are decidedly opposed to modern abolitionism, and wholly disclaim any right, wish, or intention to interfere in the civil and political relation between master and slave as it exists in the slave-holding states of this Union."

The preamble and resolutions were adopted,—the first resolution by 122 to 11, the last by 120 to 14.

An address was received from the Methodist Wesleyan Conference in England in which the anti-Christian character of slavery, and the duty of the Methodist church was plainly, yet tenderly and affectionately, presented for its consideration. The Conference refused to publish it.

In the Pastoral Address to the churches are these passages:

" It cannot be unknown to you that the question of slavery in the United States, by the constitutional compact which binds us together as a nation, is left to be regulated by the several state legislatures themselves, and thereby is put beyond the control of the general government as well as that of all ecclesiastical bodies, it being manifest that in the slave-holding states themselves the entire responsibility of its existence or non-existence rests with those state legislatures. . . . . . These facts, which are only mentioned here as a reason for the friendly admonition which we wish to give you, constrain us as your pastors who are called to watch over your souls as they must give account, to exhort you to abstain from all abolition movements and associations, and to refrain from patronizing any of their publications," &c. . . " From every view of the subject which we have been able to take, and from the most calm and dispassionate survey of the whole ground, we have come to the conclusion that the only safe, scriptural, and prudent way for us, both as ministers and people, to take, is, wholly to refrain from this agitating subject," &c.

The temper exhibited by the general conference was warmly sympathized in by many of the local conferences, not only in the slave states but in the free.

The Ohio Annual Conference had a short time before Resolved,—

" 1. That we deeply regret the proceedings of the abolitionists and Anti-Slavery Societies in the free states, and the consequent excitement produced thereby in the slave states; that we, as a Conference, disclaim all connection and coöperation with or belief in the same; and that we hereby recommend to our junior preachers, local brethren, and private members within our bounds to abstain from any connection with them, or participation of their acts in the premises whatever."

Resolved,—

"2. That those brethren and citizens of the North who resist the abolition movements with firmness and moderation, are the true friends to the church, to the slaves of the South, and to the constitution of our common country," &c.

The New York Annual Conference met in June, 1836, and

Resolved,—

"1. That this conference fully concur in the advice of the late General Conference, as expressed in their Pastoral Address."

Resolved,—

"2. That we disapprove of the members of this conference patronizing or in any way giving countenance to a paper called 'Zion's Watchman,'* because in our opinion it tends to disturb the peace and harmony of the body by sowing dissensions in the church."

Resolved,—

"3. That although we could not condemn any man or withhold our suffrages from him on account of his *opinions* merely, in reference to the subject of abolitionism, yet we are decidedly of the opinion that none ought to be elected to the office of a deacon or elder in our church, unless he give a pledge to the conference that he will refrain from agitating the church with discussions on this subject, and the more especially as the one promises 'reverently to obey them to whom the charge and government over him is committed, following with a glad mind and will, their godly admonitions:' and the other with equal solemnity, promises to 'maintain and set forward as much as lieth in him, quietness, peace, and love among all Christian people, and especially among them that are, or shall be committed to his charge.' "

In 1838 the same Conference, Resolved,—

"As the sense of this conference, that any of its members or probationers, who shall patronize Zion's Watchman, either by writing in commendation of its character, by circulating it, recommending it to our people, or procuring subscribers, or by collecting or remitting monies, shall be deemed guilty of indiscretion, and dealt with accordingly."

---

*Zion's Watchman is a newspaper devoted to the anti-slavery cause and the religious interests of the Methodist Episcopal church. It is edited by the Rev. La Roy Sunderland,

The preachers—judging by the vote on the anti-abolition resolutions—were expected of course to conform to
the advice in the pastoral address. The New York Conference, the most influential, set the example of exacting
a pledge from the candidates for orders that they would
not agitate the subject of slavery in their congregations.
The *official* newspapers of the connection would, of course,
be silent. Therefore, as a measure for wholly excluding
the slavery question from the church, it was of the last
importance that Zion's Watchman, an *unofficial* paper,
and earnest in the anti-slavery cause, should be prevented
from circulating among the members.

Having seen in what spirit the conferences of the free
states were willing to act, we will now see what was the
temper of the conferences in the slave states. *They* were
not under the same necessity as the free state conferences, of guarding against *agitation* by candidates for orders
—for in the slave states they are comparatively few, and
being brought up under the influences of slavery, are considered *sound* on that subject. The point of most interest to the slaveholding professors of religion was to *steel
their own consciences.*

The Baltimore Conference resolved :

" That in all cases of administration under the general rule in
reference to buying and [or] selling men, women, and children,
&c., it be, and hereby is recommended to all committees, as the
sense and opinion of this conference, that the said rule be taken,
construed, and understood, so as not to make the guilt or inno-
cence of the accused to depend upon the simple fact of purchase
or sale of any such slave or slaves, but upon the attendant
circumstances of cruelty, injustice, or inhumanity on the one
hand, or those of kind purposes or good intentions, on the other,
under which the transactions shall have been perpetrated; and
farther, it is recommended that in all such cases the charge be
brought for immorality, and the circumstances adduced as speci-
fications under that charge."

THE GEORGIA ANNUAL CONFERENCE.

Resolved *unanimously* that :

" Whereas, there is a clause in the discipline of our church,
which states that we are as much as ever convinced of the great
evil of *slavery ;* and whereas the said clause has been *perverted*
by some, and used in such a manner as to produce the impression
that the Methodist Episcopal church believed *slavery* to be a
moral evil."

Therefore, Resolved,—

"That it is the sense of the Georgia Annual Conference that slavery, as it exists in the United States, *is not a moral evil.*"

Resolved,—

"That we view *slavery* as a civil and domestic institution, and one with which, as ministers of Christ, we have nothing to do, further than to ameliorate the condition of the slave by endeavoring to impart to him and his master the benign influences of the religion of Christ, and aiding both on their way to Heaven."

On the motion it was resolved unanimously,—

"That the Georgia Annual Conference regard with feelings of profound respect and approbation, the dignified course pursued *by our several superintendents* or bishops *in suppressing* the attempts that have been made by various individuals to get up and protract an excitement in the churches and country on the subject of *abolitionism.*

Resolved, further,—

"That they shall have our cordial and zealous support in sustaining them in the ground they have taken."

SOUTH CAROLINA CONFERENCE.

The Rev. W. Martin introduced resolutions similar to those of the Georgia conference.

The Rev. W. Capers, D. D., after expressing his conviction that " the sentiment of the resolutions was universally held, not only by the ministers of that conference, but of the whole South ; " and after stating that the only true doctrine was, " it belongs to Cæsar, and not to the church," offered the following as a substitute :

"Whereas, we hold that the subject of slavery in these United States is not one proper for the action of the church, but is exclusively appropriate to the civil authorities,"

Therefore, Resolved,—

"That this conference will not intermeddle with it, farther than to express our regret that it has ever been introduced in any form into any one of the judicatures of the church.

" Brother Martin accepted the substitute.

" Brother Betts asked whether the substitute was intended *as implying that slavery as it exists among us was not a moral evil ? He understood it as equivalent to such a declaration.*

" Brother Capers explained *that his intention was to convey that sentiment fully and unequivocally ;* and that he had chosen the form of the substitute for the purpose, *not only of reproving some wrong doings at the North,* but with reference also to the general conference. If slavery were a *moral evil* (that is *sinful*), *the church would be bound to take cognizance of it ;* but our affirmation is that it is not a matter for *her* jurisdiction, but is exclusively appropriate to *the civil government,* and *of course not sinful.*

" The substitute was then unanimously adopted."

SENTIMENTS OF NON-SLAVEHOLDING METHODIST MINISTERS.

Rev. N. Bangs, D. D., of New York:

" It appears evident that however much the apostles might have deprecated SLAVERY as it then existed throughout the Roman empire, he did not feel it his duty, as an ambassador of Christ, to disturb those *relations* which subsisted between master and servants, by denouncing slavery as *such a mortal sin* that they could not be servants of Christ in such a relation."

Rev. E. D. Simms, Professor in Randolph Macon College, a Methodist institution :

" These extracts from HOLY WRIT UNEQUIVOCALLY ASSERT THE RIGHT OF PROPERTY IN SLAVES, together with the usual incidents of that right; such as the power of acquisition and disposition in various ways, according to municipal regulations. The right to buy and sell, and to transmit to children by way of inheritance, is clearly stated. The only restriction on the subject is in reference to the *market* in which slaves or bondsmen were to be purchased.

" Upon the whole, then, whether we consult the Jewish polity, instituted by God himself, or the uniform opinion and practice of mankind in all ages of the world, or the injunctions of the New Testament and the Moral Law, we are brought to the conclusion that slavery is not immoral.

" Having established the point that the first African slaves were legally brought into bondage, the right to detain their children in bondage follows as an indispensable consequence.

" Thus we see that the slavery which exists in America, was *founded in right.*"

The Rev. Wilbur Fisk, D. D., late President of the [Methodist] Wesleyan University in Connecticut :

" The relation of master and *slave* may, and *does, in many cases,* exist under such circumstances, as free the master from the just charge and guilt of immorality.

" 1 Cor. vii. 20-23.

" This text seems mainly to *enjoin* and *sanction* the *fitting continuance* of their present social relations: the freeman was to remain free, and the slave, unless emancipation should offer, *was to remain a slave.*

" The general rule of *Christianity* not only *permits, but in* supposable circumstances, *enjoins a continuance of the master's authority.*

" The New Testament enjoins obedience upon the slave as an obligation *due* to a present *rightful* authority."

Rev. Elijah Hedding, D. D., one of the six Methodist bishops :

"The right to hold a slave is founded on this rule, ' Therefore, all things whatsoever ye would that men should do to you, do ye even so to them : for this is the law and the prophets.' "—*Ch. Ad. and Journal, Oct.* 20, 1807.

SENTIMENTS OF SLAVEHOLDING METHODIST MINISTERS.

The Rev. William Winans, of Mississippi, in the General Conference, in 1836 :

"He was not born in a slave state—he was a Pennsylvanian by birth. He had been brought up to believe a slaveholder as great a villain as a horse-thief; but he had gone to the South, and long residence there had changed his views; he had become a slaveholder *on principle.*" . . . . "Though a slaveholder himself, no abolitionist felt more sympathy for the slave than he did; none had rejoiced more in the hope of a coming period, when the print of a slave's foot would not be seen on the soil." . . . "It was important to the interests of slaves, and in view of the question of slavery, that there be Christians who were slaveholders. Christian ministers should be slaveholders, and diffused throughout the South. Yes, sir, Presbyterians, Baptists, Methodists, should be slaveholders. Yes, he repeated it boldly, there should be members, and *deacons*, and ELDERS, and BISHOPS, too, who were slaveholders."

The Rev. J. Early, of Virginia, on the same occasion :

"SIR : We have no *energy*. But if a majority of this conference have no energy, not enough of it to protect their own honor from insult and degradation, be it known, that there are in the conference those who *have*, AND WHO OUGHT TO BE BY THEMSELVES. It is full time for you, sir, to speak *out*, to testify that you have some regard for yourselves—to say that you have some regard for your *honor*. Submit to this, sir! If we submit to this, we are prepared to submit to anything."

The Rev. J. H. Thornwell, at a public meeting held in South Carolina, supported the following resolutions :

"That slavery, as it exists in the South, is no evil, and is consistent with the principles of revealed religion ; and that all opposition to it arises from a misguided and fiendish fanaticism, which we are bound to resist in the very threshold.

"That all interference with this subject by fanatics is a violation of our civil and social rights, is unchristian and inhuman, leading necessarily to anarchy and bloodshed ; and that the instigators are murderers and assassins.

"That any interference with this subject, on the part of congress, must lead to a dissolution of the Union."

The Rev. George W. Langhorne, of North Carolina, thus writes to the editor of Zion's Watchman, under date, June 25th, 1836.

"I, sir, would as soon be found in the ranks of a banditti, as numbered with Arthur Tappan and his wanton coadjutors. Nothing is more appalling to my feelings as a man, contrary to my principles as a Christian, and *repugnant* to my soul as a *minister*, than the insidious proceedings of such men.

"If you have not resigned your credentials as a minister of the Methodist Episcopal church, I really think that, as an *honest* man, you should now do it. In your ordination vows you solemnly promised to be obedient to those who have rule over you; and since they [the General Conference] have spoken, and that distinctly, too, on this subject, and disapprobate your conduct, I conceive you are bound to submit to their authority or leave the church."

The Rev. J. C. Postell, in July, 1836, delivered an address at a public meeting at Orangeburgh Court-house, S. C., in which he maintains ; 1. That slavery is a judicial visitation. 2. That it is not a moral evil. 3. That it is supported by the Bible. He thus argues his second point :

"It is not a moral evil. The fact that slavery is of Divine appointment would be proof enough, with the Christian, that it could not be a moral evil. But when we view the hordes of savage marauders and human cannibals enslaved to lust and passion, and abandoned to idolatry and ignorance, to revolutionize them from such a state, and enslave them where they may have the gospel, and the privileges of Christians, so far from being a moral evil, *it is a merciful visitation*. If slavery was either the invention of man or a moral evil, it is logical to conclude, the power to create has the power to destroy. Why, then, has it existed? And why does it now exist amidst all the power of legislation in state and church, and the clamor of abolitionists? *It is the Lord's* DOINGS, AND MARVELLOUS IN OUR EYES, and had it not been done for the best, God alone, who is able, long since would have overruled it. IT IS BY DIVINE APPOINTMENT."

On that occasion the same Rev. gentleman read a letter which he had addressed to the editor of Zion's Watchman, of which the following are extracts :

"To La Roy Sunderland, &c.

"Did you calculate to misrepresent the Methodist Discipline, and say it supported abolitionism, when the General Conference, in their late resolutions, denounced it as a *libel on truth ?* ' *Oh full of all subtlety, thou child of the devil !'* all *liars*, saith the sacred volume, shall have their part in the lake of fire and brimstone.

"I can only give one reason why you have not been indicted for a libel. The law says, 'The greater the truth, the greater the libel ;' and as your paper has no such ingredient, it is construed but a small matter. But if you desire to educate the slaves. I will tell you how to raise the money without editing Zion's Watchman ; you and old Arthur Tappan come out to the South this winter, and they will raise one hundred thousand dollars for you. New Orleans itself will be pledged for it. Desiring no further acquaintance with you, and never expecting to see you but once in time or eternity, that is at judgment, I subscribe myself, the friend of the Bible, and the opposer of abolitionists.

"J. C. POSTELL,

"Orangeburgh, July 21st, 1836."

THE GENERAL CONFERENCE FOR 1840,

HELD ITS SESSION IN MAY, IN BALTIMORE.

The Rev. Silas Comfort appealed from a decision of the Missouri conference. of which he was a member. That conference had convicted him of "mal-administration," in admitting the testimony of a colored person in the trial of a white member of the church. The General Conference reversed the decision of the Missouri conference. The Southern delegates insisted on something being done to counteract the injurious influence which the reversal would have on the Methodist church in the slave states.

The Rev. Dr. A. J. Few, of Georgia, proposed the following:

Resolved,—

" That it is inexpedient and unjustifiable for any preacher to permit colored persons to give testimony against white persons, in any state where they are denied that privilege by law."

This was carried, but it was at variance with the decision in Comfort's case. The Conference saw the absurdity of their position, and that something must be done to shift it. To this end, it was thought best to attempt getting rid of the whole subject. A motion was made to reconsider the decision in Comfort's case, with a view, if it should be carried, to another, *not to entertain his appeal.* Should this latter prevail, a motion was then to follow, to *reconsider Dr. Few's resolution.* If this should be carried, by another motion it could be laid on the table and kept there. In this way the whole matter might be excluded.

The motion to reconsider the reversal in Comfort's case was carried. So was the motion, *not to entertain* his appeal. But the motion to reconsider *Dr. Few's resolution* failed. Pending the debate on it, one of the Southern delegates,

Rev. William A. Smith, of Virginia, [the same who, in the General Conference of 1836, publicly wished the Rev. Orange Scott, a leading abolitionist, also of the General Conference, " in heaven ;"] becoming alarmed, lest the resolution should be reconsidered and consigned to the table, offered the following compromise as a substitute :

Resolved,—

"That the resolution offered by A. J. Few, and adopted on Monday, the 18th instant, relating to the testimony of persons of color, be reconsidered and amended so as to read as follows, viz.: ' That it is *inexpedient and unjustifiable for any preacher among us to admit of persons of color to give testimony on the trial of white persons in any slaveholding state where they are denied that privilege in trials at law.* Provided, that when an annual conference in any such state or territory shall judge it expedient to admit of the introduction of such testimony within its bounds, it shall be allowed so to do.' "

However, the Southern delegates being unanimous (with the single exception of the Rev. mover), and having the aid of some of the most devoted of the pro-slavery Northern delegates, the substitute was lost by an even vote.

The efforts made to "harmonize" the slaveholding and the non-slaveholding delegates, had thus far failed. It was not, however, abandoned. With that view, Bishop Soule, acting as the representative of the other bishops, introduced three resolutions. We have not been able to procure a copy of them. In Zion's Watchman, we find them substantially stated thus :

1. " The action of the General Conference in the Comfort case was not intended to express or imply that it was either expedient or justifiable to admit the testimony of colored persons in states where such testimony is rejected by the civil authorities.

2. " It was not intended, by the adoption of Dr. Few's resolution, to prohibit the admission of it when the civil authorities or usage authorizes its admission.

3. " *Expresses the undiminished regard of the General Conference for the colored population.*"

Immediately on the passage of Dr. Few's resolution, the " official members (forty-six in number) of the Sharp

Street and Asbury Colored Methodist Episcopal Church in Baltimore," protested and petitioned against it. The following passages are in their address :

"The adoption of such a resolution by our highest ecclesiastical judicatory, a judicatory composed of the most experienced and wisest brethren in the church, the choice selection of twenty-eight annual conferences, has inflicted, we fear, an irreparable injury upon eighty thousand souls for whom Christ died—souls, who by this act of your body, have been stript of the dignity of Christians, degraded in the scale of humanity, and treated as criminals for no other reason than the color of their skin ! Your resolution has, in our humble opinion, *virtually* declared that a mere physical peculiarity, the handy work of our all-wise and benevolent Creator, is *prima facie* evidence of incompetency to tell the truth, or is an unerring indication of unworthiness to bear testimony against a fellow-being whose skin is denominated white. . . .

" Brethren, out of the abundance of the heart we have spoken. *Our grievance is before you!* If you have any regard for the salvation of the eighty thousand immortal souls committed to your care ; if you would not *thrust* beyond the pale of the church, *twenty-five hundred souls in this city*, who have felt determined never to leave the church that has nourished and brought them up ; if you regard us as children of one common Father, and can, upon reflection, sympathize with us as members of the body of Christ—if you would not incur the fearful, the tremendous responsibility of offending not only one, but many thousands of his 'little ones ;' we conjure you to wipe from your journal, the odious resolution which is ruining our people."

"A Colored Baltimorean," writing to the editor of Zion's Watchman, says :

"The address was presented to one of the secretaries, a delegate of the Baltimore conference, and subsequently given by him to the bishops. How many of the members of the conference saw it, I know not. One thing is certain, *it was not read to the conference.*"

SENTIMENTS EXPRESSED DURING THE DEBATES.

Rev. W. Capers, D. D., of Charleston, S. Carolina,

" Valued the quotations which had been made from the early disciplines and minutes ; there was no kind of property that he valued so high as the works which contained them ; they were the monuments of that primitive Methodism which he loved. ·
He then read from the minutes of 1780, '84, and '85, and attempted to show from the smallness of the church, and the little connexion that it had with slavery in 1789, that it adopted the language which was precisely consistent with its circumstances, and just such language as he would adopt under similar circum-

stances; but in 1784 and '85, when the church had extended further, and became more entangled with slavery, there was a corresponding faltering in the language of the church against it. But in 1800 the church fell into a great error on this subject—an error which he had no doubt those who were so unfortunate as to fall into, very deeply deplored. The conference authorized addresses to the legislatures, and memorials to be circulated by all our ministers, and instructed them to continue those measures from year to year, till slavery was abolished. He had no doubt that the men engaged in this work were sincere and pious, but they soon perceived that it was a great error, and abandoned it.
. . He thanked the brother from Canada (Rev. Egerton Ryerson), for the strong sympathy he had expressed for Southern institutions. . . Notwithstanding the representations that a part of the discipline was a dead letter in the South, yet he assured them that they received the whole of it—they were under the whole of it—acknowledged it all.—but, said he, you must take heed what discipline you make for us now; if the chapter on slavery had not long been in the discipline, you could not put it there now. I repeat, therefore, you must *beware* what laws you make for us ! You may easily adopt such measures as will effectually hedge up our way, and make us slaves. We cannot be made slaves; beware, therefore, I say, what discipline you give us ! Be CAUTIOUS what burthens you impose upon us ! We know what our work is,—it is to preach and pray for the slaves."

Rev. Mr. Crowder of Virginia :

" In its *civil* aspect, neither the general government, or any other government, ecclesiastical or civil, either directly or indirectly, has a right to *touch* slavery." In its *ecclesiastical* aspect, " we are bound by the twenty-third article of our religion to submit to the civil regulations of the state under which we live." In its *moral* aspect, "Slavery was not only countenanced, permitted, and regulated by the Bible, but it was positively *instituted* by GOD HIMSELF—he had in so many words ENJOINED it."

The Rev. Joshua Soule, D. D., of Ohio (one of the bishops), in advocating the reconsideration of the decision in Comfort's case, said :

" It will be recollected by brethren that the Missouri conference fixed no *censure*—not a particle of censure upon the character of Silas Comfort ; the law, therefore, would not justify an appeal to this body. If that unfortunate word '*mal-administration*,' had not been used in connection with the case, it would never have found its way here." "I do not express merely my own opinion in this case ; it is the united opinion of your superintendents (bishops), and it is by their request that I address you on this occasion."

Rev. Mr. Peck, of New York, who moved the reconsideration of Dr. Few's resolution :

" That resolution, said he, was introduced under peculiar circumstances, during considerable excitement, and he went for it as a peace-offering to the South, without sufficiently reflecting upon the precise import of its phraseology; but after a little deliberation, he was sorry, and he had been sorry but once, and that was all the time; he was convinced that, if that resolution remain upon the journal, *it would be disastrous to the whole Northern church.*"

Rev. Dr. A. J. Few of Georgia, the mover of the original resolution :

"Look at it! What do you declare to us in taking this course ? Why, simply as much as to say, ' we cannot sustain you in the condition which you cannot avoid !' We cannot sustain you in the necessary conditions of slaveholding ; one of its necessary conditions being the rejection of negro testimony. If it is not sinful to hold slaves under all circumstances, it is not sinful to hold them in the only condition, and under the only circumstances, which they can be held. The rejection of negro testimony is one of the necessary circumstances under which slaveholding can exist; indeed, it is utterly impossible for it to exist without it ; therefore it is not sinful to hold slaves in the condition and under the circumstances which they are held at the South, inasmuch as they can be held under no other circumstances. . . If you believe that slaveholding is necessarily sinful, come out with the abolitionists and honestly say so. If you believe that slaveholding is necessarily sinful, you believe we are necessarily sinners : and, if so, come out and honestly declare it, *and let us leave you.* . . We want to know distinctly, precisely, and honestly the position which you take. We cannot be tampered with by you any longer. We have had enough of it. We are tired of your sickly sympathies. . . If you are not opposed to the principles which it involves, unite with us, *like honest men,* and go home and boldly meet the consequences. We say again, you are responsible for this state of things, for it is *you* who have driven us to the alarming point where we find ourselves. . . *You* have made that resolution absolutely necessary to the quiet of the South ! But *you* now revoke that resolution ! And you pass the Rubicon ! Let me not be misunderstood. I say *you* pass the Rubicon ! If you revoke, you revoke the principle which that resolution involves, and you array the whole South against you, *and we must separate!* . . If you accede to the principles which it involves, arising from the necessity of the case, stick by it, ' though the heavens perish !' But if you persist on reconsideration, I ask in what light will your course be regarded in the South ? What will be the conclusion there, in reference to it ? Why, that you cannot sustain us as long as we hold slaves ! It will declare in the face of the sun, ' we cannot sustain you, gentlemen, while you retain your slaves !' Your opposition to the resolution is based upon your opposition to slavery ; you cannot, therefore, maintain your consistency, unless you come out with the abolitionists, and condemn us at once and forever ; or else refuse to reconsider."

The Rev. William Winans of Mississippi (the same
who was a delegate to the general conference in 1836):

"He was never more deeply impressed with the solemnity of
his situation—the act of this afternoon will determine the fate of
our beloved Zion! . . Will you meet us half way? Have you
the magnanimity to consent to a compromise? I pledge myself,
in behalf of every Southern man, that if you will affirm the decision in the case of Silas Comfort, we will give up the resolution; but if you refuse to affirm, and wrest from us that resolution, you stab us to the vitals! . . Repeal that resolution, and
you pass the Rubicon! Dear as union is, sir, there are interests
at stake in this question which are dearer than *union!* Do not
regard us as threatening! . . . But what will become of our
beloved Methodism? The interests of Methodism throughout
the whole South are at stake! We can, however, endure to see
the houses of God forsaken, and our wide-extended and beautiful
fields, which we have long been cultivating, laid waste and
turned into a moral wilderness. But what is to become of the
poor slave? I entreat of you to pause! You effectually shut out
the consolations and hopes of the gospel from hundreds and
thousands of poor slaves . . I call heaven to record against
you this day, that if you repeal that resolution, you seal the dam-
nation of thousands of souls! I beseech you as upon my knees
not to do it."

The Rev. Mr. Collins, of———,

"Admonished the conference, that the moment they rescinded
that resolution, they passed the Rubicon. The fate of the connexion was sealed."

The Rev. William A. Smith, of Virginia,

"Agreed with the brother from Mississippi, that there were interests involved in this question *dearer* than UNION itself, however dear that might be. Southerners are not prepared to commit
their interests, much less their consciences, to the holy keeping
of Northern men. *Conscience* was involved in this matter, and
they could not be coerced."

Rev. Nathan Bangs, D. D., of New York:

"We were on a snag, and he believed he could help us off.
He perceived a way to get out of the difficulty, and proceeded to
read three resolutions, one of which went to *affirm* the decision of
the Missouri conference in the Comfort case. He concluded with
a proposition to refer the *whole case* to a committee, to see if
something could not be done to *harmonize* the conference."

Rev. P. P. Sanford, of———:

"Brethren spoke as though there were no interests involved in
this question but Southern and Western, but he could assure brethren of their entire mistake. The North and East were as deeply
concerned in the issue of this question as the West and South. .
He was surprised at the course of Dr. Bangs, who, when the

Missouri case was pending, retired without the bar, and thus *dodged* the question ; and when Dr. Few's resolution was passed, he sat still in his chair, and refused to do his duty, but *now* he comes forward with a series of resolutions entirely inconsistent with all the facts in the case, with the very benevolent intention to enlighten us on the subject ! !   But what does he say? Why, he declares that he believes that this conference ought to affirm the decision of the Missouri conference in the case of Silas Comfort ! And what was that decision? Why, that it is mal-administration to admit the testimony of a *colored* man in the trial of a white man ! So that Comfort was condemned, as appears from the journals of that conference, solely for admitting the testimony of a *colored man !* And Dr. Bangs is the man who declares upon this floor, that that decision ought to be affirmed by this conference ! ! He was perfectly *astounded !* Brethren talk of compromise ! Is there any compromise in this ? "

Bishop Soule spoke in favor of the compromise resolutions of the Rev. Mr. Smith :

" It was in view of the vast but jeoparded interests of our beloved Zion : with a view to promote the union of our extended ecclesiastical confederation, that he ventured to speak on the present occasion. He would lay one hand upon the North and East, and the other upon the South, and constrain them to *harmonize.* He had listened to the speeches of brethren, and he perceived that the waters were troubled, but he was not alarmed : our ship is not wrecked, and he had no doubt but that we should bring her safe through. . . . . He had listened to the intimations of the possible necessity of adopting this measure, but brethren had approached so near together that they only appeared to differ as to the *modus operandi* of doing the thing which all seemed to agree should be done. He could not, therefore, believe that brethren were in earnest in intimating the *probability of a division* [of the church] on so *trifling* an occasion. He had heard the appeals from brethren of the South with unmingled sympathy, because he was acquainted with the South ; he was familiar with the difficulties which brethren from that region struggled with. . . We are in danger of forgetting that men born in the South are much better qualified to judge of the bearing which particular measures will have upon that region than those of the North can be. He thanked the brother from Georgia (Dr. Few) for his kind allusion to him, and regretted that he was understood to take ground against the Dr., for *he agreed with him entirely.* . . The brethren from the South came forward with all that frankness which characterizes Southern men—I say, *with all that frankness which characterizes Southern men,* for this is a distinguishing trait in their character—and propose a conciliatory plan, which he thought could not fail to *harmonize* the great majority ; I say, the great majority, for I despair of giving satisfaction to all. . . He could not possibly see an objectionable feature in, or any favorable effect that would be likely to result from, adopting them, either in the North or South. Does any one think that they may be disastrously used in the North, in favor of modern abolitionism? I neither see it nor fear it. Permit me to say to the members of this General Conference who are connected with the abolition movements, that the brethren at the South are better judges, circumstanced as they are, than you can possibly be, in regard to *every* thing connected with slavery. . . . . . Surveying the whole ground of this unfortunate affair, and where is the man who dare come to the conclusion that sufficient reasons have been developed in this controversy for dividing the body of Christ."

* THE BAPTIST CHURCH.
(500,000 *Members.*)

In 1835, the Charleston Baptist Association addressed a memorial to the legislature of South Carolina, which contains the following:

"The undersigned would further represent, that the said association does not consider that the holy scriptures have made the fact of slavery a question of morals at all. The Divine Author of our holy religion, in particular, found slavery a part of the existing institutions of society; with which, if not sinful, it was not his design to *intermeddle*, but to leave them entirely to the control of men. Adopting this, therefore, as one of the allowed arrangements of society, he made it the province of his religion only to prescribe the reciprocal duties of the relation. The question, it is believed, is purely one of political economy. It amounts, in effect, to this: *Whether the operatives of a country shall be bought and sold, and themselves become property, as in this state; or whether they shall be hirelings, and their labor only become property, as in some other states.* In other words, whether an employer may buy the whole time of laborers at once, of those who have a right to dispose of it, with a permanent relation of protection and care over them, or, whether he shall be restricted to buy it in certain portions only, subject to their control, and with no such permanent relation of care and protection. *The right of masters to dispose of the time of their slaves has been distinctly recognized by the Creator of all things,* who is surely at liberty to vest the right of property over any object in whomsoever He pleases. That the lawful possessor should retain this right at will, is no more against the laws of society and good morals, than that he should retain the personal endowments with which his Creator has blessed him, or the money and lands inherited from his ancestors, or acquired by his industry. And neither society nor individuals have any more authority to demand a relinquishment without an equivalent, in the one case than in the other.

" As it is a question purely of political economy, and one which in this country is reserved to the cognizance of the state governments severally, it is further believed that the state of South Carolina alone has the right to regulate the existence and condition of slavery within her territorial limits; and we should resist to the utmost every invasion of this right, come from what quarter and under whatever pretence it may."

In 1835, the following *query*, referring to slaves, was presented to the Savannah River Baptist Association of Ministers:

" Whether, in case of involuntary separation of such a character as to preclude all prospect of future intercourse, the parties ought to be allowed to marry again?"

Answer,—

"That such separation among persons situated as our slaves are, is *civilly* a separation by *death*, and they believe that, in the sight of God, it would be so viewed. To forbid second marriages in such cases would be to expose the parties, not only to stronger hardships and strong temptations, but to *church censure*, for acting in obedience to their masters, who cannot be expected to acquiesce in a regulation at variance with justice to the slaves, and to the spirit of that command which regulates marriage among Christians. *The slaves are not free agents*, and a dissolution by death is not more entirely without their consent, and beyond their control, than by such separation."

Sept., 1835. The ministers and messengers of the Goslien Association, assembled at Free Union, Virginia, state:

" The most of us have been born and brought up in the midst of this population. Very many of us, too, have been ushered into life under inauspicious circumstances, having no patrimonies to boast, and inheriting little else from our parents but an existence and a name. We have, however, through the blessing of God, by a persevering course of industry and rigid economy, acquired a competent support for ourselves and families; and as a reward for our laborious exertion we received such *property* [slaves] as was guaranteed to us not only by the laws of our individual states, but by those of the United States. In consideration whereof we unanimously adopt the following resolutions :"

1. Resolved,—

"That we consider our right and title to this property altogether legal and *bona fide*, and that it is a breach of the faith, pledged in the federal constitution, for our Northern brethren to try, either directly or indirectly, to lessen the value of this property or impair our title thereto."

2. Resolved,—

" That we view the torch of the incendiary and the dagger of the midnight assassin loosely concealed under the specious garb of humanity and religion falsely so called."

3. Resolved,—

"That we consider there is something radically wrong in the logic of those would-be philanthropists at the North, who lay it down as one of their main propositions that they must do what is right, regardless of consequences, inasmuch as they will not venture to come this side of the Potomac to teach and lecture publicly, where (they say) this crying evil exists."

SENTIMENTS OF INDIVIDUAL BAPTISTS.

The late Rev. Lucius Bolles, D. D., of Massachusetts, Cor. Sec. Am. Bap. Board for Foreign Missions:

(1834) "There is a pleasing degree of union among the multiplying thousands of Baptists throughout the land. . . . Our Southern brethren are generally, both ministers and people, slaveholders."

Rev. R. Furman, D. D., of South Carolina:

"The right of holding slaves is clearly established in the Holy Scriptures, both by precept and example."—*Exposition of the views of the Baptists, addressed to the Governor of S. Carolina*, 1833."

Dr. Furman died not long afterward. His legal representatives thus advertise his property for sale:

"*Notice.*

"On the first Monday of February next, will be put up at *public auction*, before the *court house*, the *following property*, belonging to the estate of the late Rev. Dr. FURMAN, viz:

"A plantation or tract of land on and in the Wataree Swamp. A tract of the first quality of fine land, on the waters of Black River. A lot of land in the town of Camden. A LIBRARY of a miscellaneous character, CHIEFLY THEOLOGICAL.

27 NEGROES,

Some of them very prime. Two mules, one horse, and an old wagon."

THE PRESBYTERIAN CHURCH.
(350,000 *Members.*)

In 1793, the General Assembly, not very long after it was organized, adopted the "judgment" of the New York and Philadelphia Synods, in favor of "universal liberty." In 1794 it adopted the following as a note to the eighth commandment, as expressing the doctrine of the church on slaveholding:

"1 Tim. i. 10. The law is made for MAN-STEALERS. This crime among the Jews exposed the perpetrators of it to capital punishment; Exodus xxi. 15: and the apostle here classes them with sinners of the first rank. The word he uses, in its original import, comprehends all who are concerned in bringing any of the human race into slavery, or *in retaining them in it. Hominum fures, qui servos vel liberos abducunt, retinent, vendunt, vel emunt.* Stealers of men are all those who bring off slaves or freemen, and KEEP, SELL, or BUY THEM. To steal a freeman, says Grotius, is the highest kind of theft. In other instances, we only steal human property, but when we steal, or retain men in slavery, we seize those who, in common with ourselves, are constituted by the original grant lords of the earth."

But the church contented itself with *recording* its doctrine. No rules of discipline were enforced. The slaveholders remained in the church, adding slave to slave, unmolested ; not only unmolested, but bearing the offices of the church. In 1816 the General Assembly, while it called slavery "a mournful evil," directed the ERASURE of the note to the eighth commandment. In 1818, it adopted an "EXPRESSION OF VIEWS," in which slavery is called "a *gross violation* of the most precious and sacred *rights* of human nature," but instead of requiring the instant abandonment of this "*violation of rights*," the Assembly exhorts the *violators* "to *continue* and increase their *exertions* to effect a *total* abolition of slavery, with no greater *delay* than a regard to the public welfare *demands;*" and recommends that if a "*Christian professor* shall sell a slave who is also in communion with our church," without the consent of the slave, the seller should be "suspended till he should repent and make *reparation*."

The *reality* of slavery in the Presbyterian church, since 1818, may be known from the following testimonies :

The Rev. James Smylie, A. M., of the Amite Presbytery, Mississippi, in a pamphlet published by him a short time ago in favor of American slavery, says :

"If slavery be a sin, and advertising and apprehending slaves, with a view to restore them to their masters, is a direct violation of the Divine law, and if *the buying, selling, or holding a slave* FOR THE SAKE OF GAIN, is a heinous sin and scandal, then, verily, THREE-FOURTHS OF ALL THE EPISCOPALIANS, METHODISTS, BAPTISTS, and PRESBYTERIANS in ELEVEN STATES OF THE UNION, are of the devil. They 'hold,' if they do not buy and sell slaves, and, *with few exceptions*, they hesitate not to 'apprehend and restore' runaway slaves, when in their power."

In 1834 the Synod of Kentucky appointed a committee of twelve to report on the condition, &c., of the slaves. This passage occurs in the report :

"Brutal stripes and all the various kinds of personal indignities are not the only species of cruelty which slavery licenses. The law does not recognise the family relations of the slave, and extends to him no protection in the enjoyment of domestic endearments. The members of a slave family may be forcibly separated so that they shall never more meet until the final judgment. And cupidity often induces the masters to practise what the law allows. Brothers and sisters, parents and children, husbands and wives are torn asunder, and permitted to see each other no more. *These acts are daily occurring in the midst of us.* The shrieks and the agony, often witnessed on such occasions, proclaim with a trumpet-tongue the iniquity and cruelty of our system. The cries of these sufferers go up to the ears of the Lord of Sabaoth. There is not a neighborhood where these heart-rending scenes are not displayed. There is not a village or road that does not behold the sad procession of manacled outcasts, whose chains and mournful countenances tell that they are exiled by force from all that their hearts hold dear. Our church, years ago, raised its voice of solemn warning against this flagrant violation of every principle of mercy, justice, and humanity. Yet we blush to announce to you and to the world that this warning has been often disregarded, even by those who hold to our communion. *Cases have occurred in our own denomination where professors of the religion of mercy have torn the mother from her children, and sent her into a merciless and returnless exile.* Yet acts of discipline have rarely [*never*] followed such conduct."

In 1835, Mr. Stewart, of Illinois, a ruling elder, in a speech urging the General Assembly of which he was a member, to *act* on the subject of slavery, bears this testimony to the existing state of things in the Presbyterian church :

" I hope this Assembly are prepared to come out fully and declare their sentiments, that slaveholding is a most flagrant and heinous SIN. Let us not pass it by in this indirect way, while so many thousands and tens of thousands of our fellow-creatures are writhing under the lash, often inflicted too, by ministers and elders of the Presbyterian church. . . . .

" In this church, a man may take a free-born child, force it away from its parents, to whom God gave it in charge, saying, ' Bring it up for me,' and sell it as a beast or hold it in perpetual bondage, and not only escape corporeal punishment, but really be esteemed an excellent Christian. Nay, even ministers of the gospel, and Doctors of Divinity, may engage in this unholy traffic, and yet sustain their high and holy calling. . . . .

" Elders, ministers, and Doctors of Divinity are, with both hands, engaged in the practice."

The speech from which the above is extracted, was made in support of various memorials and petitions from members of the Presbyterian church, asking that the General Assembly might proceed to carry out its principles as they were avowed in 1794 and in 1818. Nothing was done this session, further than to refer all such memorials and petitions to a committee (a majority of whom were known to be opposed to the prayer of the memorialists), to report at the next session in 1836.

At the meeting of the Assembly in 1836, the first thing that was done, to conciliate the excited slaveholders, was to elect one of them to be *Moderator*.

The majority of the committee appointed in 1835, of which the Rev. Samuel Miller, D. D., and theological professor, was chairman, did accordingly report at the session of 1836, as follows:

"That after the most mature deliberation, which they have been able to bestow on the interesting and important question referred to them, they would most respectfully recommend to the General Assembly, the adoption of the following preamble and resolution:

" Whereas, the subject of slavery is inseparably connected with the laws of many of the states in this Union, with which it is by no means proper for an ecclesiastical judicature to interfere, and involves many considerations in regard to which great diversity of opinion and intensity of feeling, are known to exist in the churches represented in this Assembly : And whereas, there is great reason to believe, that any action on the part of this Assembly in reference to this subject, would tend to distract and divide our churches, and would probably, in no wise promote the benefit of those whose welfare is immediately contemplated in the memorials in question,"

Therefore, Resolved,—

1. "That it is not expedient for the Assembly to take any further order in relation to this subject.

2. "That as the *notes* which have been expunged from our public formularies, and which some of the memorials referred to the committee request to have restored, were introduced irregularly—never had the sanction of the church—and therefore, never possessed any authority—the General Assembly has no power, nor would they think it expedient to assign them a place in the authorized standards of the church."

The minority of the committee, the Reverend Messrs. Dickey and Beman, reported the following resolutions:

Resolved,—

1. "That the buying, selling, or holding a human being as property, is in the sight of God a heinous sin, and ought to subject the doer of it to the censures of the church.

2. "That it is the duty of every one, and especially of every Christian, who may be involved in this sin, to free himself from its entanglement without delay.

3. "That it is the duty of every one, especially of every Christian, in the meekness and firmness of the gospel, to plead the cause

of the poor and needy by testifying against the principle and practice of slaveholding; and to use his best endeavors to deliver the church of God from the evil; and to bring about the emancipation of the slaves in these United States, and throughout the world."

The slaveholding delegates to the number of forty-eight, met *apart*, and Resolved,—

"That if the General Assembly shall undertake to exercise authority on the subject of slavery, so as to make it an immorality, or shall in any way declare that Christians are criminal in holding slaves, that a declaration shall be presented by the Southern delegation, declining their jurisdiction in the case, and our determination not to submit to such decision."

At an adjourned meeting they adopted the following preamble and resolution, to be presented in the Assembly, as a substitute for those of Dr. Miller:—

"Whereas the subject of slavery is inseparably connected with the laws of many of the states of this Union, in which it exists under the sanction of said laws, and of the Constitution of the United States; and whereas, slavery is recognized in both the Old and New Testaments as an existing relation, and is not condemned by the authority of God: therefore, Resolved,—The General Assembly have no authority to assume or exercise jurisdiction in regard to the existence of slavery."

The whole subject was finally disposed of by the adoption of the following preamble and resolution:—

"Inasmuch as the Constitution of the Presbyterian church, in its preliminary and fundamental principles, declares that no church judicatories ought to pretend to make laws to bind the conscience *in virtue of their own authority;* and as the urgency of the business of the Assembly, and the shortness of the time during which they can continue in session, render it impossible to deliberate and decide judiciously on the subject of slavery in its relation to the church: therefore, Resolved,—That this whole subject be indefinitely postponed."

A large number of memorials and petitions went up to the General Assembly of 1837. They were referred to a committee of which the Rev. Dr. Witherspoon, a slaveholder of South Carolina—the same who was moderator the year before—was chairman. After detaining them till nearly the usual time for the final adjournment of the Assembly, he reported that "the committee had had a number of papers submitted to them from various Synods, churches, and individuals, men and women, on the subject of slavery: and the committee had unanimously agreed (with the exception of a single member) to direct that they be returned to the house, and that he should move to lay the whole subject on the table," which was accordingly done by a vote of 97 to 28.

In 1838 the Presbyterian church separated on doctrinal differences. Instead of one General Assembly, there are now two, known as the "Old School" and the "New School." In the *convention*, which was held by the Old School preparatory to separation, it was Resolved,—

"That in the judgment of this convention, it is of the greatest consequence to the best interests of our church that the subject of slavery shall not be agitated or discussed in the sessions of the ensuing General Assembly, and if any motion shall be made, or resolution offered touching the same, this Convention is of opinion that the members of Convention in that body ought to unite in disposing of it, as far as may be possible, without debate."

Since the separation the course of the Old School has been regulated by the spirit of this resolution.. It has done nothing on the subject.

Petitions and memorials against slavery were presented in the New School Assembly at its first session in 1838, and referred to a committee which reported "that the applicants, for reasons satisfactory to themselves, have withdrawn their papers." The committee was discharged.

In 1839 it referred the whole subject to the Presbyteries, to do what they might deem advisable.

In 1840 a large number of memorials and petitions against slavery were sent in, and referred to the usual committee. The committee reported a resolution, referring to what had been done last year, declaring it *inexpedient for the Assembly to do anything further on the subject.* Several attempts were made by the abolition members of the Assembly to obtain a decided expression of its views, but they proved ineffectual, and the whole subject was *indefinitely postponed.* Why, it may be asked, especially by those who at the time the separation took place flattered themselves that the New School would show itself *really* opposed to slavery,—Why has such a result been brought about? The answer is plain: The New School Assembly is more solicitous to have the favor of the few slaveholders who are members, than to have the blessings of the poor who are perishing in their grasp ; more earnest to equal the Old School in numbers than to outstrip it in righteousness.

SENTIMENTS OF PRESBYTERIES AND SYNODS.

Although many of the influential Presbyterian ministers in the free states, especially in the cities and large towns, have shown themselves ready to second the slaveholding ministers and laymen in their opposition to abolitionism, from some cause it has happened that the free state Presbyteries and Synods have not committed themselves *directly* on the question. They have attempted to stay the progress of abolitionism by resolutions bearing on it *indirectly.*—but well understood by those who were to act under them as intended to exclude, as far as was safe, the question of abolition from the churches.

The following resolutions were passed by Presbyteries and Synods in slave states :—

HOPEWELL PRESBYTERY, SOUTH CAROLINA.

1. "Slavery has existed in the church of God from the time of Abraham to this day. Members of the church of God have held slaves bought with their money, and born in their houses: and this relation is not only recognized, but its duties are defined clearly, both in the Old and New Testaments.

2. "Emancipation is not mentioned among the duties of the master to his slave, while obedience, 'even to the froward' master, is enjoined upon the slave.

3. "No instance can be produced of an otherwise orderly Christian being REPROVED, much less EXCOMMUNICATED from the church, for the single act of holding domestic slaves, from the days of Abraham down to the date of the modern abolitionist."

HARMONY PRESBYTERY OF SOUTH CAROLINA.

"*Whereas.* Sundry persons in Scotland and England, and others in the North, East, and West of our country, have denounced slavery as obnoxious to the laws of God, some of whom have presented before the general assembly of our church and the congress of the nation memorials and petitions, with the avowed object of bringing into disgrace slaveholders, and abolishing the relation of master and slave; *and whereas,* from the said proceedings, and the statements, reasonings, and circumstances connected therewith, it is most manifest that those persons 'know not what they say, nor whereof they affirm,' and with this ignorance discover a spirit of self-righteousness and exclusive sanctity," &c. ;—

Therefore, 1. Resolved,—

"That as the kingdom of our Lord is not of this world, His church, as such, has no right to abolish, alter, or effect any institution or ordinance of men, political or civil," &c.

2. Resolved:—"That slavery has existed from the days of those good old slaveholders and patriarchs, Abraham, Isaac, and Jacob, (who are now in the kingdom of heaven) to the time when the Apostle Paul sent a run-away home to his master, Philemon, and wrote a Christian and fraternal letter to this slaveholder, which we find still stands in the canon of the Scriptures—and that slavery has existed ever since the days of the Apostle, and does now exist."

3. Resolved:—"That as the relative duties of master and slave are taught in the Scriptures, in the same manner as those of parent and child, and husband and wife, the existence of slavery itself is not opposed to the will of God; and whosoever has a conscience too tender to recognize this relation as lawful, is 'righteous over much,' is 'wise above what is written,' and has submitted his neck to the yoke of men, sacrificed his Christian liberty of conscience, and leaves the infallible word of God for the fancies and doctrines of men."

CHARLESTON UNION PRESBYTERY.

"It is a principle which meets the views of this body, that slavery, as it exists among us, is a political institution with which ecclesiastical judicatories have not the smallest right to interfere; and in relation to which any such interference, especially at the present momentous crisis, would be *morally wrong*, and fraught with the most dangerous and pernicious consequences. The sentiments which *we* maintain, *in common with Christians at the South of every denomination*, are sentiments which so fully approve themselves to our consciences, are so identified with our solemn convictions of duty, that we should maintain them under any circumstances."

Resolved,—

"That in the opinion of this Presbytery, the holding of slaves, so far from being a SIN in the sight of God, is no where condemned in his holy word—that it is in accordance with the example, or consistent with the precepts of patriarchs, apostles, and prophets, and that it is compatible with the most fraternal regard to the best good of those servants whom God may have committed to our charge; and that, therefore, they who assume the contrary position, and lay it down as a fundamental principle in morals and religion, that all slaveholding is wrong, proceed upon false principles."

SYNOD OF SOUTH CAROLINA AND GEORGIA.

Resolved, unanimously,—[Dec., 1834].

"That in the opinion of this synod, abolition societies, and the principles on which they are founded in the United States, are inconsistent with the interests of the slaves, the rights of the holders, and the great principles of our political institution."

SYNOD OF VIRGINIA.

The committee to whom were referred the resolutions, &c., have according to order, had the same under consideration—and respectfully report that in their judgment the following resolutions are necessary and proper to be adopted by the Synod at the present time:

Whereas, the publications and proceedings of certain organized associations, commonly called anti-slavery, or abolition societies, which have arisen in some parts of our land, have greatly disturbed and are still greatly disturbing the peace of the church and of the country ; and the Synod of Virginia deem it a solemn duty which they owe to themselves and to the community to declare their sentiments upon the subject; therefore,

Resolved, unanimously,—

" That we consider the dogma fiercely promulgated by said associations—that slavery as it exists in our slaveholding states is necessarily sinful, and ought to be immediately abolished, and the conclusions which naturally follow from that dogma, as directly and palpably contrary to the plainest principles of common sense and common humanity, and to the clearest authority of the word of God."

The above are all of the Old School. The following is from a slaveholding New School church, in Petersburg, Virginia (16th Nov., 1838) :—

" Whereas, the General Assembly did, in the year 1818, pass a law which contains provisions for slaves, irreconcilable with our civil institutions, and solemnly declaring slavery to be sin against God—a law at once offensive and insulting to the whole Southern community,"

1. Resolved,—

" That, as slaveholders, we cannot consent longer to remain in connection with any church where there exists a statute conferring the right upon slaves to arraign their masters before the judicatory of the church—*and that too for the act of selling them without their consent first had and obtained.*"

2. Resolved,—

" That as the Great Head of the church has recognized the relation of *master and slave*, we conscientiously believe that slavery is not a sin against God as declared by the General Assembly."

3. Resolved,—

"That there is no tyranny more oppressive than that which is sometimes sanctioned by the operation of ecclesiastical law."

SENTIMENTS OF PRESBYTERIAN MINISTERS.

The Rev. Gardiner Spring, D. D., of New York:

At the anniversary of the American Colonization Society at the city of Washington, in 1839, this gentleman appeared on the platform as one of the speakers, with Mr.

Henry D. Wise (M. C.), of Virginia, a slaveholder and professed duelist. The latter had said in his speech, *the best way to meet the abolitionists was* with *"Dupont's best"* [gunpowder] *and cold steel.* The *Sun*, one of the New York city journals, tells us—the Rev. Doctor *spoke with sympathy of the sentiments of the South as evinced in the speech of Mr. Wise.*

Since this, Dr. S. has preached a series of sermons to his congregation on slavery in its scriptural relations. These sermons have been printed, and are looked on by the pro-slavery party as highly serviceable to their cause.

The Rev. Joel Parker, D. D., President of the Presbyterian Theological Seminary, New York:

"Abolitionism might be pronounced a sin as well as slavery."

This was said, according to the American papers, at the last session of the (N. S.) General Assembly, in supporting the proposition of a slaveholder, that "all action on the subject of slavery, should be declared by that body beyond its relations and functions."

The Rev. Dr. P., at the beginning of the anti-slavery movement in the United States, was an abolitionist. He was sent to New Orleans, being thought eminently fitted as a Christian minister, to contend against the prevailing iniquities of that slaveholding city. He had not been there long, before he became a *colonizationist.* He happened to be at Alton, Illinois, at the time the mob spirit was beginning to show its bloody intents toward the Rev. Mr. Lovejoy. His injurious remarks in public against the abolitionists were thought to have contributed to excite the mob to the fatal issue which took place. He afterwards returned to New York; was elected pastor of the Tabernacle church, of which Mr. Lewis Tappan was a member; resisted the formation by that gentleman of an anti-slavery society among the members of the church; prosecuted Mr. T. before the church session, on various charges, with a view of ejecting him from the church, and has, generally, since his return to New York, distinguished himself by bitterness of spirit and language against the anti-slavery cause. *Since all which,* he has been made a D. D. and President of the (N. S.) Theological Seminary in New York.

The Rev. Samuel H. Cox, D. D., of the city of Brooklyn, moved the indefinite postponement of the slavery question at the last (N. S.) General Assembly. On the motion being carried he exultingly said, "Our Vesuvius is safely capped for three years"—the Assembly not meeting again till 1843. Dr. Cox was at one time an abolitionist.

The Rev. William S. Plummer, D. D., of Richmond:

[This gentleman is the leader of the Old School party. He was absent from Richmond at the time the clergy in that city purged themselves in a body, from the charge of being favorably disposed to abolition. [See page 14.] On his return, he lost no time in communicating to the "Chairman of the Committee of Correspondence," his agreement with his clerical brethen. The passages quoted occur in his letter to the chairman.]

"I have carefully watched this matter from its earliest existence, and everything I have seen or heard of its character, both from its patrons and its enemies, has confirmed me, beyond repentance, in the belief, that, let the character of Abolitionists be what it may, in the sight of the Judge of all the earth this is the most meddlesome, impudent, reckless, fierce, and wicked excitement I ever saw.

"If Abolitionists will set the country in a blaze, it is but fair that they should receive the first warming at the fire.

"Let it be proclaimed throughout the nation that every movement made by the fanatics (so far as it has any effect in the South) does but rivet every fetter of the bondsman—diminish the probability of anything being successfully undertaken for making him either fit for freedom or likely to obtain it. We have the authority of Montesquieu, Burke, and Coleridge, three eminent masters of the science of human nature, that of all men slaveholders are the most jealous of their liberties. One of Pennsylvania's most gifted sons has lately pronounced the South the *cradle of liberty*.

"Lastly—Abolitionists are like infidels, wholly unaddicted to martyrdom for opinion's sake. Let them understand that *they will be caught* [lynched] if they come among us, and they will take good heed to keep out of our way. There is not one man among them who has any more idea of shedding his blood in this cause than he has of making war on the Grand Turk."

Rev. Thomas S. Witherspoon, of Alabama, writing to the editor of the *Emancipator:*

"I draw my warrant from the scriptures of the Old and New Testaments to hold the slave in bondage. The principle of holding the heathen in bondage is recognized by God. . . . When the tardy process of the law is too long in redressing our grievances, we of the South have adopted the summary remedy of

Judge Lynch; and really, I think it one of the most wholesome and salutary remedies for the malady of Northern fanaticism that can be applied, and no doubt my worthy friend, the editor of the Emancipator and Human Rights, would feel the better of its enforcement, provided he had a Southern administrator. I go to the Bible for my warrant in all moral matters. . . Let your emissaries dare venture to cross the Potomac, and I cannot promise you that their fate will be less than Haman's. Then beware how you goad an insulted, but magnanimous people to deeds of desperation."

Rev. Robert N. Anderson, of Virginia:

"To the Sessions of the Presbyterian Congregations within the bounds of the West Hanover Presbytery:"

"At the approaching stated meeting of our Presbytery, I design to offer a preamble and string of resolutions on the subject of the use of wine in the Lord's Supper; and also a preamble and string of resolutions on the subject of the treasonable and abominably wicked interference of the Northern and Eastern fanatics, with our political and civil rights, our property, and our domestic concerns. You are aware that our clergy, whether with or without reason, are more suspected by the public, than the clergy of other denominations. Now, *dear Christian brethren*, I humbly express it as my earnest wish, that you *quit yourselves like men*. If there be any stray goat of a minister among you, tainted with the blood-hound principles of abolitionism, let him be ferreted out, silenced, excommunicated, and left to the *public to dispose of him in other respects.*

"Your affectionate brother in the Lord,
ROBERT N. ANDERSON."

THE PROTESTANT EPISCOPAL CHURCH.

The number of members in this church is not known. It is, however, small when compared with the number in any of the churches that have been mentioned. Its congregations are mostly in the cities and towns, and they generally consist of persons in the wealthier classes of society. This, together with the smallness of its numbers and the *authority* of the bishops, has prevented it from being much agitated with the anti-slavery question. Its leading ministers, so far as they concern themselves at all about the slavery question, are in favor of the American colonization scheme. Their influence is, therefore, decidedly adverse to emancipation. The prevailing temper of the Protestant Episcopal church is thus testified of by John Jay, Esq., of the city of New York, himself an Episcopalian, in a pamphlet entitled, "Thoughts on the duty of the Episcopal church in relation to Slavery:"

"Alas! for the expectation that she would conform to the spirit of her ancient mother! She has not merely remained a mute and careless spectator of this great conflict of truth and justice with hypocrisy and cruelty, but her very *priests and deacons may be seen ministering at the altar of slavery,* offering their talents and influence at its unholy shrine, and openly repeating the awful blasphemy, *that the precepts of our Saviour sanction the system of American slavery.* Her Northern (free State) clergy, with rare exceptions, whatever they may feel upon this subject, rebuke it neither in public nor in private; and her periodicals, far from advancing the progress of abolition, at times oppose our societies, impliedly defending slavery, as not incompatible with Christianity, and occasionally *withholding* information useful to the cause of freedom."

Although apparently desirous of keeping clear of all connection with the anti-slavery movement, the Episcopalians have not failed when a suitable opportunity presented itself to throw their influence against it.

The Rev. Peter Williams, rector of St. Philip's church, New York, a colored gentlemen, was one of the executive committee of the American Anti-Slavery Society, in 1834, when the abolitionists were exposed in their persons and property to the fiercest onsets of pro-slavery mobs. The Bishop of the diocese (Rev. Benjamin F. Onderdonk, D. D.) required of Mr. Williams to relinquish his place in the committee, to which requisition Mr. W. thought it his duty to conform.

Bishop Bowen, of Charleston, South Carolina, not long after the meeting in that city, in which the "reverend gentlemen of the clergy," had so handsomely and unanimously "responded to public sentiment," volunteered in an address to the Convention of his diocese, a denunciation of the "malignant philanthropy of abolition," and contrasted "the savageism and outlawry consequent on abolition," with "domestic servitude under the benign influence of Christian principles and Christian institutions!"—principles and institutions which denied Sunday School instruction to free colored children, and which, at the very time of the Address, tolerated the offer in the *Charleston Courier* of *fifty dollars for the* HEAD *of a fugitive slave*—principles and institutions which led Mr. Preston to declare in his place as a Senator of the United States, "Let an abolitionist come within the borders of South Carolina—if we can catch him we will hang him."

In 1836, a clergyman in North Carolina, of the name of Freeman, preached in the presence of his bishop (Rev. Levi S. Ives, D. D , a native of a free state), two sermons on the rights and duties of slaveholders. In these he essayed to justify from the Bible the slavery both of white men and negroes, and insisted that "without a new revelation from heaven no man was authorized to pronounce slavery *wrong*." The sermons were printed in a pamphlet, prefaced with a letter to Mr. Freeman from the bishop of North Carolina, declaring that he had "listened with most unfeigned pleasure" to his discourses, and advised their publication as being "urgently called for at the present time."

"The Protestant Episcopal Society for the advancement of Christianity in South Carolina" thought it expedient, and in all likelihood with Bishop Bowen's approbation, to republish Mr. Freeman's pamphlet as *a religious tract!*"

The Churchman is edited by a Doctor of Divinity, late an instructor in a theological seminary, and enjoys the especial patronage of the Bishop of New York, and was recently officially recommended by him to the favor of the convention. The editor has frequently assailed the abolitionists in his columns in bitter and contemptuous terms. He has even volunteered to defend the most cruel and iniquitous enactment of the slave code. In reference to the legal prohibition of teaching the colored population to read, the editor says :

"All the knowledge which is necessary to salvation, all the knowledge of our duty toward God, and our duty toward our neighbor, may be communicated by oral instruction, and therefore a law of the land interdicting other means of instruction does not trench upon the law of God."

A certain congregation in the diocese of New York is said to hold its cemetery by a tenure which forbids the interment of any colored person ; so that if an Episcopal colored clergyman happen to die in that parish, he would be indebted to others than his Episcopal brethren for a grave !

There are instances of regularly ordained ministers, rectors of parishes, men having as valid a commission to preach the gospel as any other presbyters in the Episcopal church, who are virtually denied a seat in her Ecclesiastical councils, *solely because they are men of color.* The rector of a colored church in Philadelphia, is excluded by an express canon of the Diocesan Convention.

"THE GENERAL THEOLOGICAL SEMINARY OF THE PROTESTANT EPISCOPAL CHURCH IN THE UNITED STATES," is in the city of New York. It is called the *General* Seminary, because it is under the superintendence of the whole church ; the board of trustees being composed of the Bishops, *ex-officio*, and upwards of one hundred clerical and lay gentlemen, representing the different states and territories of the Union. It was intended, of course, for the theological education of the Protestant Episcopal ministry.

Alexander Crummel, a colored young gentleman of New York, made application to become a "candidate for holy orders" in the church, and was duly admitted as such. In due time Mr. Crummel received from the Bishop of the diocese the usual circular in such cases, in which he was told "unless you belong to the General Theological Seminary, as it is my wish that all the candidates of this diocese should, when not prevented by unavoidable circumstances, you will be governed," &c.

The section in the statutes of the seminary regulating admission is plain and imperative :—"Every person producing to the *faculty* satisfactory evidence of his *having been admitted* a candidate for holy orders," &c., "shall be received as a student of the seminary."

It does not appear from the only account we have at hand, of this matter, that Mr. Crummel made application to the faculty. It is, however, to be presumed he did, and that the faculty put him off by referring him to the board of trustees. To the board, then, he made his application, of which an account is given in the following

EXTRACT FROM THE MINUTES:

Tuesday, June 25th, 1839.

"A communication from Mr. Crummel, asking admission to the Seminary as a student, was read, and on motion referred to a Committee consisting of the following gentlemen, appointed by the chair : Right Rev. Bishop Doane, Rev. Drs. Milnor, Taylor, and Smith, Messrs. D. B. Ogden, Newton, and Johnson."

June 26th, 1839.

"The Right Rev. Bishop Doane, chairman of the committee on the petition of Mr. Crummel, asked to be relieved from further service on that committee, which request was granted.

"The Right Rev. Bishop Onderdonk, of Pennsylvania, was on motion appointed chairman of the committee, to fill the vacancy thus occasioned."

June 27th, 1839.

"The committee on the petition of Mr. Crummel, submitted the following:

"The committee to whom was referred the petition of Mr. Crummel, respectfully report, that having *deliberately* considered the said petition, they are of opinion that it ought not to be granted, and they accordingly recommend to the Board of Trustees the following resolution : Resolved, That the prayer of the petitioner be not granted.

"The Rev. Dr. Hawks,* moved that the resolution recommended in the report be adopted."

Mr. Huntington moved,—

"That the whole subject be recommitted, with instructions to the committee to report, that the matters embraced in the petition of Mr. Crummel are, according to Section 1, of Chap. VII. of the Statutes, referrible to the faculty rather than this board."

[This motion was lost, through fear, we are constrained to believe, lest the faculty would not, if *compelled* to act, refuse to Mr. Crummel a right that was so obviously his.]

"Whereupon the question upon accepting the report and adopting the resolution recommended, was taken up and decided in the affirmative.

"The Right Rev. Bishop Doane gave notice, that he should, on the morrow, ask leave to present to the board, and to enter upon the minutes a *protest* against the decision.

Friday, June 28th.

"The Right Rev. Bishop Doane, who had yesterday given notice of his intention to ask leave to enter a protest, &c., changed his intention as to the manner of presenting the subject, and asked leave to state to the board his reasons, with a view to the entering of the same on the minutes, for dissenting from the vote of the majority on the report of the committee, to whom was referred the petition of Mr. Crummel. *Leave was not granted.*"

During these proceedings, attempts were made by the Bishop of New York to prevail on Mr. Crummel to withdraw his application for admission, by assuring him "the members of the faculty were willing to impart to him [*private*] instruction in their respective departments ; and that more evil than benefit would result both to the church and himself, by a formal application in his behalf for admission into the seminary."

* Dr. Hawks is the *Historian* of the Episcopal church in the United States. If it be true, as we have seen stated in an American newspaper, that this gentleman is himself of mixed blood—and his *complexion* a little favors the statement—it proves that the admixture does not deteriorate the intellectual powers; for in the oratory of the pulpit, and as a writer, Dr. H. stands, deservedly, among the distinguished men of America.

48

The reader will not have failed to notice with what care every allusion to the *cause* of refusing Mr. Crummel admission is excluded from the minutes, and to feel that the very fact that the cause does *not* appear in the minutes—leaving it to be inferred, that it was for something too base to be recorded there—is an act of injustice to him that admits of no excuse.*

"*An Episcopalian*" of New York, jealous for the honor of his church, published in one of the journals of that city, a full account of these proceedings. The Bishop of New York made a short reply to but one of his statements (an immaterial one), and concluded by saying, that *in the discharge of his duties and responsibilities, he should not certainly be swayed by any appeal that might be made to popular feeling.*

POSTSCRIPT.

We would have the reader bear in mind, that the foregoing presents but one side of the anti-slavery cause in the several churches whose proceedings have been considered; and that in them all, there are abolitionists earnestly laboring to purify them from the defilements of slavery; and that they have strong encouragement to proceed, not only in view of what they have already effected toward that end, but in the steady increase of their numbers, and in other omens of success.

We wish him also to bear in mind, that the churches which have been brought before him are not the only American churches which are guilty in giving their countenance and support to slavery. Of others we have said nothing, simply because, to examine their cases, would be to make this work too long for the object we have in view—and because enough has been said to show substantially the state of the slavery question in America, so far as the CHURCH in that country is connected with it.

Lastly.—We take pleasure in assuring him that there are considerable portions of the Methodist, Baptist, and Presbyterian churches, as well as the entire of some of the smaller religious bodies in America, that maintain a commendable testimony against slavery and its abominations.

* Mr. Crummel became a member of the Theological department of Yale College, a Congregational institution, where we wish we could say he was there treated in a manner that would have been the most agreeable to him, as well as most honorable to the *distinguished* professor whose lectures he attended; but we cannot.